MILITARY MIGHT

space∞ ™

Business Leaders

Engineering Wonders

Extreme Survival

Feats of Courage

Hacking for Good

Incredible Comebacks

Military Might

Sports Superstitions

Unusual Jobs

Women in Combat

Wrongly Accused

SADDLEBACK
EDUCATIONAL PUBLISHING
www.sdlback.com

Photo credits: page 10: AFP/DDP via Getty Images; page 11: Uriel Sinai/Getty Images News via Getty Images; pages 12/13: AB Forces News Collection/Alamy Stock Photo; page 14: Dondi Tawatao/Getty Images News via Getty Images; pages 16/17: Getty Images News via Getty Images; page 18: Corbis Historical via Getty Images; page 20: Getty Images/Hulton Archive via Getty Images; pages 24/25: Karolis Kavolelis/Shutterstock.com; page 26: Chip Somodevilla/Getty Images News via Getty Images; page 27: The Mariner 4291/Shutterstock.com; pages 28/29: USAF/Getty Images News via Getty Images; page 30 (top to bottom): Mai/The LIFE Images Collection via Getty Images; Angel DiBilio/Shutterstock.com; page 31: E Alchowiak/Moment via Getty Images; page 36: Brian Blanco/Getty Images News via Getty Images; pages 38/39: Gado Images/Stockbyte via Getty Images; pages 40-41: Mike Mareen/Shutterstock.com; page 42: John Moore/Getty Images News via Getty Images; page 43: Justin Sullivan/Getty Images News via Getty Images; page 48: George Rinhart/Corbis Historical via Getty Images; page 52: Getty Images News via Getty Images; page 53: U.S. Navy/Getty Images News via Getty Images

ISBN: 978-1-68021-752-0
eBook: 978-1-64598-058-2

Printed in Malaysia

26 25 24 23 22   1 2 3 4 5

TABLE OF CONTENTS

CHAPTER 1
THE ARMED FORCES

Low rumbles fill the air. The ground shakes. Clouds
of dust appear. A tank roars into view and stops.
Inside, the crew prepares for battle.

A soldier grabs the heavy hatch. Pulling it down, he
takes his seat. There is barely any room to move inside.
Sweat drips down his face. He wipes his eyes and looks
outside. It is dangerous. **Mines** could explode at any
time.

Another soldier searches for the target. **Ammunition** is
close by. A third soldier loads it into the large gun. The
commander shouts instructions. It is time.

Soldiers check the weapon's aim. They fire. Lights flash
and smoke rises from the gun. Rounds of ammo shoot
out. Enemy troops fire **shells** that crash around the
tank. The crew hopes its armor will keep them safe.

FIVE BRANCHES OF THE ARMED FORCES

The United States has the most powerful military in the world. U.S. forces protect American citizens. Five branches make up the armed forces. The U.S. Air Force rules the sky. On land, the Army takes charge. Oceans are protected by the Navy. Marine Corps soldiers attack from water, land, or air. The Coast Guard patrols waterways.

All military branches use mighty machines. Every year, billions of dollars are spent. The money is used for weapons and vehicles. Improvements are made. Jets fly faster. Guns are more precise. Trucks are made safer. Technology changes quickly. New inventions come out all the time.

MILITARY INVENTIONS

Many useful inventions have come from the military. They were first developed for soldiers to use. Later, some of this technology was passed on to civilians.

The Global Positioning System (GPS) was a military invention. Today, cell phones use this technology. It shows people where they are on a map and helps them find where they want to go. At first, the Navy used GPS. In the 1960s, they used it to locate submarines.

Military leaders needed a way to share information. Computers were connected. They used wires. These attached to phone lines. Information could be shared. Later, the system didn't need wires. This led to the internet.

In the 1940s, a scientist was standing next to a military radar system. He felt heat. It melted food in his pocket. The scientist shared what he found. Engineers started working on microwaves. Two years later, the first microwave ovens were sold to the public.

CHAPTER 2
FIREARMS

Soldiers use firearms in battle. These weapons can be held. They include rifles. Handguns are also firearms. Machine guns are too.

Some guns have been used for a long time. Army troops still use the M2 Browning. This machine gun was invented in 1933. It is powerful. The gun lets soldiers fire bullets quickly.

Smart guns use technology. Computers make them more accurate. The TrackingPoint smart rifle collects data. It measures a target. A system in the gun tracks the target. Information is sent to a phone or computer.

Then a program does math. The distance between the gun and target is measured. A computer finds the best shot. This means soldiers do not need as much training. They hit their mark more often. Even from far away, the rifle is accurate. It can hit a target from more than half a mile away.

ARMATIX PISTOL

Another smart gun is the Armatix pistol. A soldier wears a watch. This lets her fire the weapon. The gun and watch share a signal. It has to match. Only the watch can unlock the gun. Her gun might fall into the wrong hands. But it cannot be used without the watch. Information is recorded on the watch too. This includes shots fired.

Since the 1960s, the military has used the M16 rifle. The gun is accurate and lightweight. This makes it easy to use. It became the main rifle used in battle.

There is a newer version. It is called the M4 **carbine**. This gun is shorter and lighter. With ammunition, it weighs seven pounds. Soldiers can carry it easily.

The M4 can be used at close range. Even at a distance, the gun is still accurate. Its range is almost 2,000 feet. Sand may be a problem. Dust can be an issue too. Both get into the weapon. Then it cannot shoot. Engineers are working to find a solution.

CORNER SHOT

The Corner Shot is an accessory for guns. It attaches to a pistol. The front part holds the small gun. There is also a camera attached.

A soldier holds the back part of the Corner Shot. There is a monitor. It shows the soldier what the camera sees. The whole system bends in the middle. Then the weapon can be fired around corners. This helps soldiers stay hidden, especially when shooting around buildings.

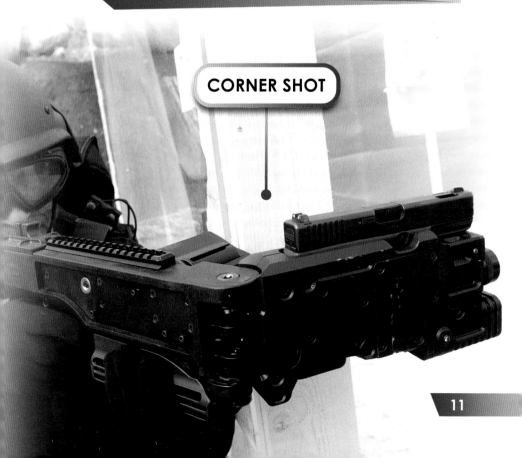

CORNER SHOT

CHAPTER 3
ARTILLERY

Artillery are heavy guns. Many have a long range. Certain guns are very large. Trucks have to move them. Cannons are big weapons. Rocket launchers are too. Others are smaller. Soldiers carry these. The guns are set on the ground. Then they can be fired.

Mortars have been used in combat for hundreds of years. These are big guns. Many are four to five feet long. They fire short-range bombs. Modern mortars are lightweight. Soldiers fire them from **trenches**. Their **trajectory** is high.

In 2016, a new mortar came out. It is the Advanced Capability Extended Range Mortar (ACERM). ACERM has a longer range. Its bombs land six miles away. M252 mortars were used before. Their range was around 3.5 miles. Wings were added to ACERM's bombs. GPS guides them. This makes the bombs more accurate.

ADVANCED CAPABILITY
EXTENDED RANGE MORTAR

The M109 Howitzer is a special gun. It is self-propelled. This weapon sits on a truck. A soldier drives it onto the battlefield.

M109s were first used in the 1960s. Their range has gotten better since then. They can fire faster too. Howitzers are 30 feet long. This is the size of a small tank. Four crew members control it. Shells travel 18 miles away. Engineers want to increase the range. The goal is 43 miles.

HIMARS is a rocket launcher. This stands for High Mobility Artillery Rocket System. It can be moved between places. A fast vehicle carries it. The weapon usually holds six rockets. Missiles can be carried too. Soldiers fire them. Then HIMARS races away. Enemies cannot find the truck. This speed protects the crew. Armor can be added to the vehicle too.

HIGH MOBILITY ARTILLERY ROCKET SYSTEM

ELECTROMAGNETIC RAILGUN

The electromagnetic railgun is a cannon. Navy scientists are testing it. This gun has massive strength. It launches bombs at a speed of more than 4,500 miles per hour. These bombs travel for 100 miles. Scientists are improving the weapon. They want it to fire ten shots per minute.

These guns use electricity. It flows between two metal rails. A bomb sits between them. Magnetic force pushes the bomb. It explodes out of the gun. There is one problem though. The force is too strong. With every shot, the gun is damaged. Engineers are working to fix this.

HOW AN ELECTROMAGNETIC RAILGUN WORKS

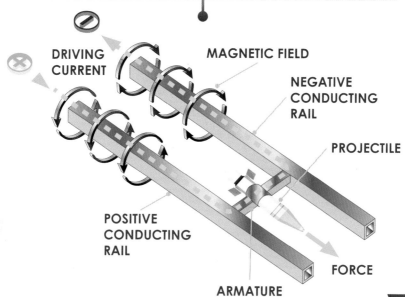

DRIVING CURRENT

MAGNETIC FIELD

NEGATIVE CONDUCTING RAIL

PROJECTILE

POSITIVE CONDUCTING RAIL

FORCE

ARMATURE

CHAPTER 4
MISSILES

Missiles are weapons. They are launched into the air. Short-range missiles travel less than 100 miles. Long-range ones can go over 3,000 miles. A few reach almost 10,000 miles. These missiles can land on other continents.

Ships launch missiles. Submarines carry them too. They are also fired from planes. Ballistic missiles are sent high into the air. Gravity pulls them back down. Cruise missiles are guided. These fly very low. Soldiers direct where they land.

The Navy uses Tomahawks. These are cruise missiles. Ships and submarines carry them. Tomahawks hit targets on land. They go far. Their range is 1,000 miles.

Tomahawks are fast. Their top speed is 550 miles per hour (mph). GPS guides them. The missiles are 20 feet long. A 1,000-pound bomb can also be attached.

Fighter jets use the AIM-9 Sidewinder. This missile has a short range. It only travels about ten miles. An **infrared** system directs it. This means it finds heat. Targets can be in the air. Some are on land. Others are at sea.

Sidewinders have been used since the 1950s. They work very well. The system was improved in 2003. Missiles are better at finding targets. It is also harder for enemies to find the weapons.

TOMAHAWK MISSILE

THREE PHASES OF FLIGHT FOR BALLISTIC MISSILES

A ballistic missile goes through three phases of flight.

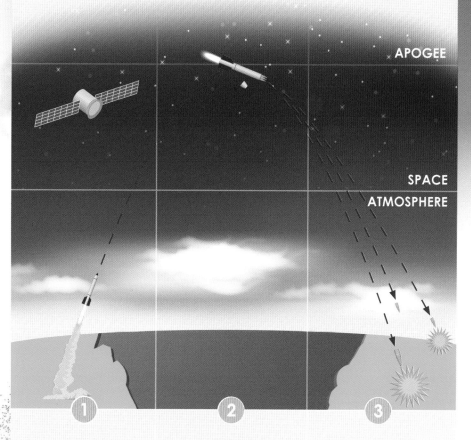

APOGEE

SPACE
ATMOSPHERE

1 BOOST PHASE
The first phase is called boost. Rockets push the missile. It gains speed.

2 MIDCOURSE PHASE
Midcourse is next. Rockets use all their power. The missile is still going up. It reaches its apogee. That is its highest point. Then the missile starts to fall. This phase lasts the longest.

3 TERMINAL PHASE
Terminal is the final phase. The missile falls back to Earth. Weapons fly off the missile. They head toward targets.

TRIDENT MISSILE

Subs carry Trident missiles. Nuclear warheads are inside. Tridents are powerful. Their top speed is 20,000 feet per second. The range is more than 7,500 miles. These weapons are accurate. They land within a few feet of a target.

Trident missiles help prevent nuclear war. Other countries know they could be used. This keeps them from using their own nuclear weapons. These missiles have never been fired in war.

HYPERSONIC MISSILES

The fastest missiles are supersonic. Mach 2 or 3 are their highest speeds. Engineers are making hypersonic ones. They will travel five times the speed of sound. Some may be even faster.

A hypersonic missile would be accurate. It could hit a target anywhere in the world. The missile would get there in one hour.

These missiles are hard to locate. They are too fast. Nothing can destroy them. China and Russia are working on them. The United States is developing these weapons too.

CHAPTER 5
ARMORED VEHICLES

Armored vehicles help keep soldiers safe in battle. Some carry troops and guns. Others protect soldiers from bombs. Tanks have heavy armor. Big guns sit on top.

The British Army was the first to use the word *tank*. This was during World War I. Their goal was to trick the enemy. Enemies might see plans for the vehicle. But they would think it was a tank that held water.

Main battle tanks (MBTs) are used for combat. A tank's armor protects its crew. Soldiers can fire directly at enemies. One MBT is the M1 Abrams. The U.S. Army uses many in battle.

MBTs are medium-sized tanks. The M1 weighs more than 60 tons. That is more than two buses. This tank travels up to 42 mph. Four people are needed to work it.

M1 ABRAMS

M1s have been used since the early 1980s. Many upgrades have been made. Computer programs are now used. They help with operations. The armor is thicker too. It is more than twice as dense as steel.

In 2018, the Army decided to make a change. Each tank would have an anti-missile system. This shoots down rockets. Then they cannot hit the tanks.

The BFV rides over rough ground. This is the Bradley Fighting Vehicle. Three crew members run it. A commander is in charge. There is a **gunner** too. Another soldier drives. Computer systems help **navigate**. The BFV can also move six soldiers. It has more room inside than a tank.

BFVs have been used since 1981. Automatic cannons were added later. The vehicle can launch anti-tank or anti-aircraft missiles too.

BRADLEY FIGHTING VEHICLE

Clearing bombs is dangerous. The Buffalo MRAP vehicle finds them. MRAP stands for Mine-Resistant Ambush Protected. It moves bombs out of the way. A claw on the front digs. Bombs are then removed.

An MRAP protects its crew. Its shape is like a V. Bomb blasts are forced away. Harnesses hold soldiers in place. The MRAP can roll over. Soldiers stay safe inside. It can transport them through dangerous areas.

BUFFALO MINE-RESISTANT AMBUSH PROTECTED VEHICLE

AMPHIBIOUS ASSAULT VEHICLE

AMPHIBIOUS ASSAULT VEHICLES

Amphibious assault vehicles (AAVs) go from water to land. These vehicles are used for attacks. In water, they float like boats. Then they drive onto the beach. A grenade launcher is their main weapon. Machine guns are also used. AAVs fight on coasts. They carry troops from ship to shore. The U.S. Marine Corps uses them. Three crew members are in charge. Up to 25 Marines ride along.

The first AAVs were slow in water. This was in the 1930s. Their top speed was only 2.5 mph. It was easier to drive them on land. Modern AAVs move 8 mph in water. They reach 45 mph on roads.

the first military branch to use airplanes. Two people fit inside. The plane could only fly for one hour at a time. New pilots used it for training.

Now all military branches use aircraft. Jets are very powerful. Certain ones are **supersonic**. Some move troops around the world. Others are used to spy on enemies. Many fly in combat. They are used to drop bombs or fire missiles at targets.

F-22 RAPTOR

Air Force pilots fly the F-22 Raptor. This jet reaches fast speeds. Its top speed is Mach 2.25. That is 2.25 times the speed of sound.

The small **cockpit** is high-tech. There are computer systems inside. They take up space. Most jets have two pilots. Only one operates the Raptor. There is no room for a copilot. Pilots have to be well trained. No one can help them fly.

A Raptor's outside is curved. The shape confuses **radar**. It bounces in different directions. This lets the planes sneak into battle.

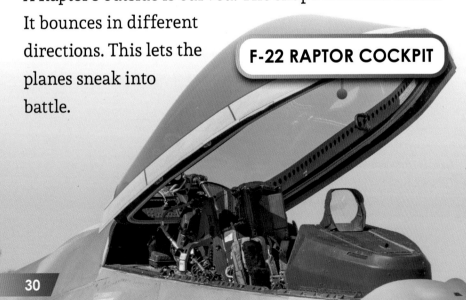

F-22 RAPTOR COCKPIT

Stealth fighters are good at hiding. The F-35 Lightning II is one. It carries out many missions. These include spying and fighting. Pilots wear special helmets. Information shows up on their visors.

Weapons are usually kept inside. This keeps the jet in "stealth" mode. Radar cannot pick it up. Outside weapons can be attached. It becomes more powerful. Then the jet is in "beast" mode.

F-35 LIGHTNING II

F-35 LIGHTNING II VERTICAL LANDING

F-35s are **agile**. They land on short runways. A vertical landing can be done too. The jets land on aircraft carriers. These ships are in the ocean.

B-21 Raiders are stealth bombers. These jets are being tested. The Air Force wants to use them by 2025. The B-21 will do long-distance missions. It will carry weapons on board. Some will be nuclear. Raiders will be almost invisible to radar. Their exact top speed is a secret.

SPY PLANES

The SR-71 Blackbird was the military's fastest plane. It flew at speeds over Mach 3. Enemies shot missiles at the jet. It did not fire back. Zooming away was its best defense.

In the 1990s, the Air Force retired Blackbirds. The National Aeronautics and Space Administration (NASA) then used the planes for research missions. In 2019, there was a new plan. It was for a spy plane. The SR-72 will be twice as fast. Speeds of Mach 6 will be possible. This is called hypersonic speed. Crossing any continent in the plane will take around one hour.

snow. They are one of the most successful helicopters in war.

BLACK HAWK HELICOPTER WITH SKIS

Apaches are the Army's main attack helicopters. They are hard to fly. The pilot uses both hands and both feet. Training takes a year and a half. Then pilots are combat-ready.

Night sensors help when it is dark. Crews launch missiles. Soldiers fire cannons. Heavy damage hurts enemies. The Apache survives most attacks. All sides are armored. It is like a flying tank.

THE KILLER EGG

The Little Bird is a light attack helicopter. It is small. Another name for it is the "Killer Egg." One or two pilots fly this chopper. A pilot can also operate it remotely, which makes unmanned flights possible.

This helicopter flies special operations. It lands in narrow spaces that would be too small for other helicopters. Three soldiers sit on benches attached to the outside. Troops are dropped off. They perform important missions.

LITTLE BIRD

The CH-53E Super Stallion is big. It is a **cargo** helicopter. Three engines move its seven blades. They create strong winds. Its nickname is "Hurricane Maker."

This helicopter lifts an armored vehicle. The weight is 30,000 pounds. Then the chopper carries it 50 miles. Inside, it also holds supplies. They can weigh 27,000 pounds. Stallions may carry troops instead of supplies. Up to 55 soldiers can fit inside.

Crew members use machine guns. They protect the cargo. A Super Stallion is heavy. But it is still fast. The top speed is 196 mph. That is faster than many tornadoes.

CH-53E SUPER STALLION

CHAPTER 8
DRONES

Drones are unmanned **aerial** vehicles. They are called
UAVs. These machines fly in the sky. Pilots run them
from the ground. Computers can control them too.
UAVs can be a few inches long. Others are the size of
jets.

UAVs fly in dangerous areas. The military uses them
for special missions. These are too risky for soldiers.
Many UAVs zoom over the battlefield. They can drop
weapons. Others spy on enemies. Information is sent
to troops.

A Black Hornet Nano is a small drone. It can fit in a hand or pocket. This UAV helps troops who are on the move. The Nano flies ahead. A camera records what it sees. Soldiers watch what is happening on a monitor. Hidden dangers are shown.

Staying hidden from the enemy is easy. This drone is almost silent. Its top speed is 11 mph. The UAV is not hard to control. Training only takes 20 minutes.

MQ-9 REAPER DRONE

MQ-9 Reaper drones do many jobs. First they were used for spying. The Reaper also does combat missions. It launches bombs and missiles. Lasers guide these weapons. Reapers can stay in the air for 34 hours. This helps the drones on long missions. These drones are the size of small jets. Two people are needed to run one. They work from the ground.

The MQ-9 can also be used for spying. Flying for up to 20 hours is possible. People called controllers operate it. They do not have to be nearby. Often they are halfway around the world.

Engineers wanted to improve the MQ-9. They created Avenger drones. These are the size of a jet. The UAVs are 41 feet long. This makes them the biggest military drones. Their top speed is 460 mph. The military made the vehicle for combat. It holds many types of bombs.

MILITARY ROBOTS

The military uses advanced robots. Some are like small tanks. They take explosive devices into battle.

Other robots spy on targets. They can look like jets. Certain ones appear to be insects. These robots record video and collect information in battles. Search and rescue is another mission. Robots can go places soldiers can't reach.

In a war zone, robots defuse bombs. Soldiers cannot do the job. It is too dangerous. These robots are on wheels. They have mechanical arms. A robot looks for bombs. Then it fires water at wires on the object. This keeps the bomb from going off.

CHAPTER 9
SUBMARINES

The U.S. Navy uses three types of submarines. One kind carries ballistic missiles. Another has cruise missiles. Fast-attack subs are used in combat. There are around 70 subs in the Navy. They can also be called boats. Subs are never called ships.

Subs stay underwater. They do this for two to three months. Running out of air is not a problem. The engine uses water from the sea to make more air. There is room for 90 days of food. All U.S. subs run on nuclear power. This helps them stay **submerged** longer.

Many sailors are needed. More than 100 crew members live on board. There are no windows. Crews look through **periscopes**. These help them see things near the surface. **Sonar** is used deep underwater.

In 2019, the U.S.S. *South Dakota* was the newest sub. This boat is part of the Virginia class. These are fast-attack subs. Sailors must be ready for combat. Weapons are on board. There are dozens of Tomahawk missiles. These are launched onto land. Torpedoes speed through the water. Crew members can use deadly mines. They set them on the ocean floor.

INTERIOR OF AN OHIO-CLASS SUBMARINE

All U.S. subs have three main sections: an operations (or forward) compartment, a reactor compartment, and an engine room. Additionally, Ohio-class subs have a missile compartment.

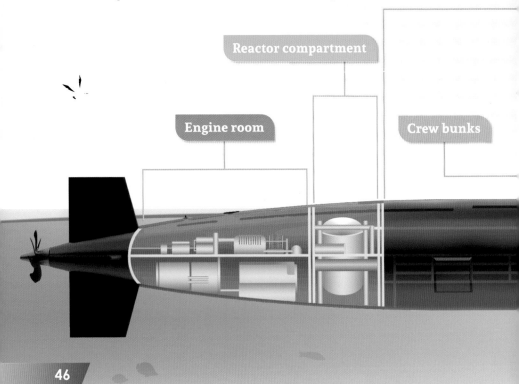

Reactor compartment

Engine room

Crew bunks

Ohio-class boats patrol silently. These are the Navy's largest subs. The boats do not enter direct combat. Instead, they have one important job. Nuclear warheads are on board. Other countries have nuclear weapons too. All countries avoid using them. But if enemies attacked, these boats would fight back.

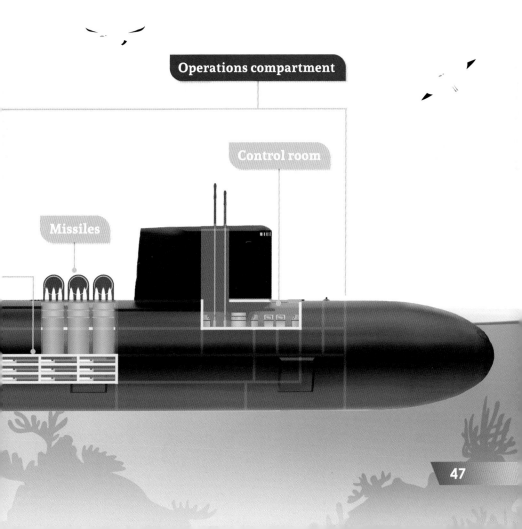

Operations compartment

Control room

Missiles

U.S.S. *SEAWOLF*

Seawolf-class subs are powerful. Up to 50 Tomahawk missiles can be on board. The subs are fast and quiet. They travel at speeds of 40 mph. Sailors carry out secret missions. A Seawolf's "official" depth is 800 feet. People believe they can dive 1,600 feet.

These subs are expensive to build. They cost around $5 billion each. Only three have been made. One is the U.S.S. *Seawolf*. Another is the U.S.S. *Connecticut*. U.S.S. *Jimmy Carter* is the third. The Navy wants to create a new submarine. It would be similar to the U.S.S. *Seawolf*.

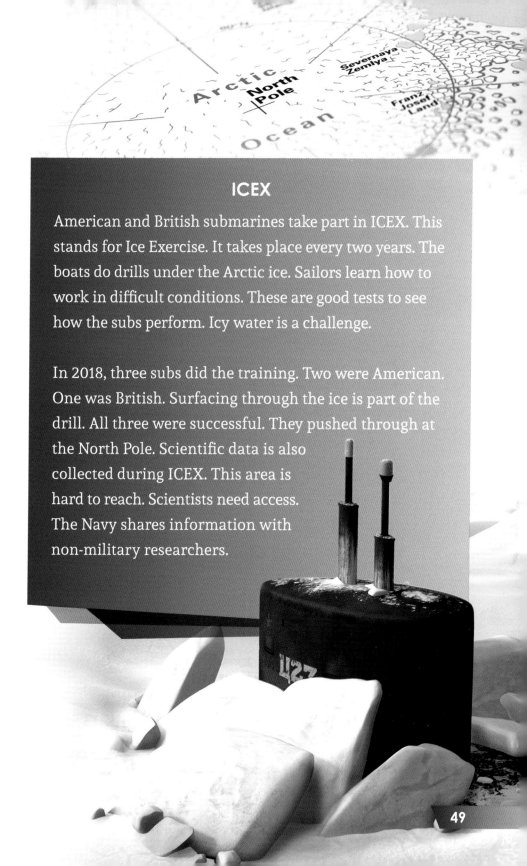

ICEX

American and British submarines take part in ICEX. This stands for Ice Exercise. It takes place every two years. The boats do drills under the Arctic ice. Sailors learn how to work in difficult conditions. These are good tests to see how the subs perform. Icy water is a challenge.

In 2018, three subs did the training. Two were American. One was British. Surfacing through the ice is part of the drill. All three were successful. They pushed through at the North Pole. Scientific data is also collected during ICEX. This area is hard to reach. Scientists need access. The Navy shares information with non-military researchers.

CHAPTER 10
SHIPS

The U.S. Navy has a long history. It began with the Revolutionary War. Ships went to battle. Then the war ended. They were not needed anymore.

It was 1794. George Washington was president. He had six new boats built. The fleet had a mission. They would fight pirates. This was the first permanent U.S. Navy. By the end of 2021, the Navy expects to have 305 ships. There is a goal to grow to 355 by 2049.

U.S.S. ZUMWALT

The Zumwalt-class destroyer is a battleship. This is the largest destroyer in the world. It attacks other boats.

Most of the ship sits below the waterline. On radar, the *Zumwalt* looks like a fishing boat. Enemies cannot find it.

The ship's crew is small for its size. About 150 sailors run it. Similar boats have 300 to 350 crew members. Computer systems have taken over some of the work.

Aircraft carriers are warships. They are floating air bases. Helicopters land on them. Huge jets can too. The U.S.S. *Gerald Ford* is the biggest. This ship joined the fleet in 2017. About 5,000 workers helped build it. Up to 75 aircraft can be on board.

NAVY HOSPITAL SHIPS

The U.S. Navy has two hospital ships. One is the *Comfort*. The other is named *Mercy*. Each is more than ten stories high. Both are the length of three football fields.

More than 1,200 crew members are needed. Civilians work on the ships too. Workers can help up to 1,000 patients at a time.

These ships wait at a dock. A small crew stays on board. They set sail when needed. Military nurses and doctors treat injured people. The patients can come from any country.

Helicopters land on the ships. They bring people who need help. People may be rescued directly from the sea. Crew members can bring them on board. Ports open on the side.

Hospital ships also assist after natural disasters. They stay away from combat. Patients must be protected.

U.S.N.S. *COMFORT*

Littoral combat ships (LCSs) fight too. They are used near the shore. If needed, LCSs join battles in the open ocean. Clearing ocean mines is another job. Other military boats can then pass through.

U.S.S. *Freedom* is an LCS. The boat's **hull** has a special design. Its surface is smooth. This keeps the boat from getting stuck in shallow waters.

A fast stream of water moves the boat. This is called a waterjet. The ship can move fast. Its top speed is 54 mph. Waterjets stop the vessel quickly if needed.

U.S.S. *FREEDOM*

The U.S. has the most advanced military in the world. Every year, engineers make better machines. A long-range cannon is planned. Robot tanks will go into battle. In the future, mighty machines could replace soldiers completely. Better weapons keep the armed forces strong. People are safe at home and overseas.

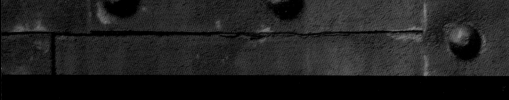

GLOSSARY

AERIAL
in the sky

AGILE
able to move quickly and easily

AMMUNITION
bullets and other objects that are shot from weapons

CARBINE
a small rifle

CARGO
equipment carried by boat or plane

COCKPIT
the part of a plane where the pilot sits

GUNNER
a soldier who operates a large gun

HULL
the outer part of a ship or boat

INFRARED
producing rays of light that cannot be seen

MINE
a bomb that goes off when triggered by touch, pressure, or
some other disturbance

NAVIGATE
to find one's way when traveling in a vehicle

PERISCOPE
a long tube that allows a person to see above the water

RADAR
radio waves that help locate objects and track speeds

SHELL
a metal ball that is full of explosive material from a mortar or other gun

SONAR
a machine that finds objects underwater using sound waves

STEALTH
a way of moving that makes something difficult to detect

SUBMERGE
to go under the surface of the water

SUPERSONIC
able to travel faster than the speed of sound

TRAJECTORY
the path along which something moves through the air

TRENCH
a hole dug by soldiers for protection

ENGINEERING WONDERS

CHAPTER 3
SKYSCRAPERS

Buildings used to be much shorter. Large cities needed a lot of land. Engineering has gotten better. Structures can be taller. More people can fit on less land. The biggest cities in the world show this. They are home to some of the tallest structures.

The tallest building in the world is the Burj Khalifa. It is 2,716 feet high. That is taller than 135 two-story houses. This building is in Dubai.

Construction began in 2004. Plans were complicated. Wind was a problem. Fast winds can make a tall building sway. People might get sick if it sways too much. Parts of a building can fall off. Engineers made the Burj Khalifa narrow. This lets the wind pass by. They gave the building rounded corners. The wind can blow without pushing it.

BURJ KHALIFA

12

13

THE TEN TALLEST U.S. BUILDINGS

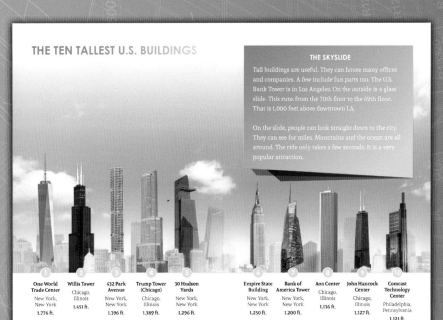

THE SKYSLIDE

Tall buildings are useful. They can house many offices and companies. A few include fun parts too. The U.S. Bank Tower is in Los Angeles. On the outside is a glass slide. This runs from the 70th floor to the 69th floor. That is 1,000 feet above downtown LA.

On the slide, people can look straight down to the city. They can see for miles. Mountains and the ocean are all around. The ride only takes a few seconds. It is a very popular attraction.

One World Trade Center	Willis Tower	432 Park Avenue	Trump Tower (Chicago)	30 Hudson Yards	Empire State Building	Bank of America Tower	Aon Center	John Hancock Center	Comcast Technology Center
New York, New York	Chicago, Illinois	New York, New York	Chicago, Illinois	New York, New York	New York, New York	New York, New York	Chicago, Illinois	Chicago, Illinois	Philadelphia, Pennsylvania
1,776 ft.	1,451 ft.	1,396 ft.	1,389 ft.	1,296 ft.	1,250 ft.	1,200 ft.	1,136 ft.	1,127 ft.	1,121 ft.

Companies want to put humans in space too. One of the leaders is SpaceX. By May 2020, the company had done 88 space launches. It was the first company to have a vehicle return from space. In May 2020, SpaceX had another first. The company sent people to the ISS. No private company had done this before.

Space vehicles are difficult to **design**. They must be safe. On Earth, the **atmosphere** protects people. It keeps the sun from being too strong. Off the planet, there is no protection. **Materials** must be tough. Detailed planning is needed. SpaceX engineers and scientists are working on these problems.

ENGINEER ELON MUSK

Elon Musk is a famous engineer. He has created many innovative projects. Musk created Tesla. This company makes luxury cars. They are electric.

Musk is also behind SpaceX. He wants to put people on Mars. That will take advanced technology and design.

This engineer sets big goals for himself and for humankind. Musk wants cars to be self-driving. He also wants to provide cheap trips to the moon. That way, anyone can visit it. To reach these goals, engineering wonders will be needed.

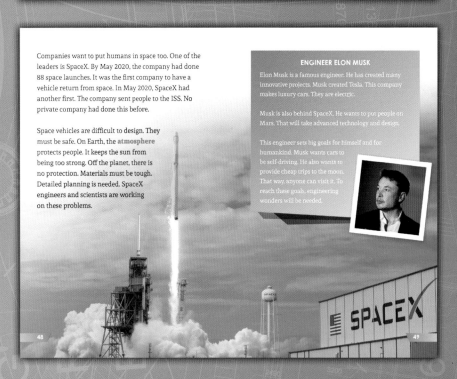

FOR MORE TITLES AND INFORMATION →

space∞™

BUSINESS LEADERS

9781680217513

ENGINEERING WONDERS

9781680217575

EXTREME SURVIVAL

9781680217483

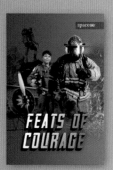

FEATS OF COURAGE

9781680217476

HACKING FOR GOOD

9781680217469

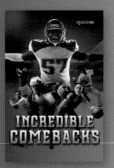

INCREDIBLE COMEBACKS

9781680217490

MILITARY MIGHT

9781680217520

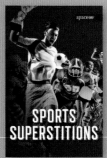

SPORTS SUPERSTITIONS

9781680217445

UNUSUAL JOBS

9781680217568

WOMEN IN COMBAT

9781680217506

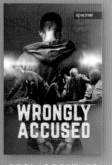

WRONGLY ACCUSED

9781680217452

MORE TITLES COMING SOON
sdlback.com/Space-8